MW01195843

21 Days of Powerful Breakthroughs

Kemberley Washington, CPA

@kemwashcpa

www.21daysof.com

DEDICATION

I dedicate this book to D and Jay for simply reading
everything I write!

Table of Contents

Foreword

It is amazing how God works. I decided to start a fast, knowing in His Word some things only come by fasting and praying. I had no intentions of writing a book. As a matter of fact, I wrote daily using my smartphone as thoughts came to me. I always enjoyed writing, so I decided I would write passages to encourage myself. As I continued to write, the Spirit of God encouraged me to share my writing with friends and to create a book for others.

I have to tell you these last twenty-one days have been powerful. Along with this fast came many tests, but more importantly, powerful breakthroughs. There were some issues God has worked out on my behalf. There were attacks of evil that were stopped dead in its tracks. Relationships were restored, healings performed, financial blessings occurred and I surrendered all to God and obtained a peace I desired.

During my journey, not only did I write but also I prayed three times a day for long periods of time. I would often wake in the middle of the night and pray. Whenever you are facing big issues, you have to do a big thing for God. I was also given a scripture from a friend of the family during this time, which I recited throughout the fast:

"Blotting out the handwriting of ordinances that was against us, which was contrary to us, and took it out of the way, nailing it to his cross; And

*having spoiled principalities and
powers, He made a shew of them openly,
triumphing over them in it."
(Colossians 2:14-15, King James Version)*

Everyday, I believed the things that have come
against me would be nailed to the cross! I
envisioned each issue being nailed and, more
importantly, I cast it there knowing God would
take care of these issues for me. And He did!

I want to thank everyone who has been so helpful
to me during this fast. I especially want to thank
my siblings and best friends for providing me with
feedback and reading each daily devotional as I
wrote them. I especially want to thank my parents
for helping me as a young person to build a
relationship with God.

It is my expectation that this fast would also be as
much a blessing to you as it was for me. No
matter what, stand on His Word, He is faithful
and powerful. Continue to give Him praise even
during trials and you will see they will indeed turn
around for you. No matter what, continue to run
the good race until you have obtained His
promises!

*"Know ye not that they which run in a
race run all, but one receiveth the
prize? So run, that ye may obtain."
(1 Corinthians 9:24)*

Introduction

I want you to declare and decree (Proverbs 18:21), at the end of this fast, the issues you have been worrying about for such a long time will no longer worry you anymore.

Starting now, I want you to begin proclaiming God is giving you peace, healing, tranquility, and serenity at this very moment.

I want you now to begin to give God all the things you have worried about for so long and begin to cast your cares upon Him (1 Peter 5:7). The word *cast* is defined as something being changed into a suitable form. As we cast our cares upon Him, we can believe He is changing them into a useful form, which would be used for our good (Romans 8:28).

Start envisioning yourself lifting every issue to heaven and more importantly allowing it to remain until God has resolved your issue or transformed it to a form you are able to use.

Day 1 - The Lord will see us through

Scripture Reading: "So that we may boldly say, The Lord is my helper, and I will not fear what man shall do unto me."

(Hebrews 13:6)

Do you understand how powerful this scripture is? We know no matter who has plotted against us; God promises to help us through! Whether on our job, within our relationships, or while in school, we can trust God is there to help us (Hebrews 13:6). We do not have to be fearful because God has already promised victory.

Daily Prayer: Heavenly Father, we come to You today worshipping You in spirit and truth (John 4:23-24). We thank You that we do not have to fear our enemies, anyone who comes against us on our jobs or those desiring to destroy our relationships because we know no weapon formed against us shall prosper (Isaiah 54:17). We thank You for removing worrying regarding these issues from our minds, hearts, bodies and souls. We know in the end, all things work together for our good (Romans 8:28) and the battle is not ours but Yours (2 Chronicles 20:15). We rejoice now because we know You will show up and show out and make our enemies our footstool (Luke 20:43). In the name of Jesus Christ of Nazareth, we pray (John 14:14). Amen.

Reflection: Think about a time you worried about an issue and God gave you victory. Remember, He is the same God yesterday, today and tomorrow (Hebrews 13:8)! He will for certain help you once again!

Notes:

_____
_____
_____
_____
_____
_____
_____
_____
_____
_____
_____
_____
_____
_____
_____
_____
_____
_____
_____
_____
_____
_____
_____
_____
_____
_____
_____
_____
_____
_____
_____
_____
_____

Day 2 - Worry not, pray always

Scripture Reading: "But seek ye first the kingdom of God, and His righteousness; and all these things shall be added unto you."

(Matthew 6:33)

For so often, many of the battles we are worrying about are things God never intended for our lives. We must begin to adopt a mindset to seek Him first prior to making any decisions on our own. You have to begin to ask yourself, "Is this God approved?" In James 1:12, it tells us when a man has been approved, he will receive the crown of life, which the Lord has promised to anyone who loves Him.

Let God lead you

Before you begin your day, turn on the news, or get the kids ready for school, take time to ask God for His guidance. Ask Him to guide your decisions, thoughts, words and mindset, so you can live the life God has purposed for you!

It will not grieve you

Then and only then, you may go through trials and tribulations but it will not grieve you (1 Chronicles 4:10). You will find yourself with a sense of peace (John 14:27) neglecting to worry, blessed day in and day out, and living a fulfilled life because each decision has already been pre-approved by God!

Daily Prayer: Heavenly Father, we come to You today worshipping You in spirit and truth (John 4:23-24).

We are committed today to seek You first and to obey Your commandments. We declare and decree blessings will begin to chase us. God, for this very reason, we know we do not have to worry, because You have gone before us and made all the crooked places straight (Isaiah 45:2). Lord, anything that has been designed for evil has already been turned around for our good (Romans 8:28). In the name of Jesus Christ of Nazareth, we thank You for powerful breakthroughs and lifting worrying off of our minds. We know we can stand on Your Word because You are providing us with a way out and a way through, just as You did with Moses and the Red Sea (Exodus 14:16). We pray every decision we make this day has God's stamp of approval. In the name of Jesus Christ of Nazareth, we pray (John 14:14). Amen.

Reflection: Reflect on a time when you sought God's guidance and how the situation worked out for your good. Remember, He promises to be your shepherd so you will want for nothing (Psalm 23:1).

Notes:

_____
_____
_____
_____
_____
_____
_____
_____
_____
_____
_____
_____
_____
_____
_____
_____
_____
_____
_____
_____
_____
_____
_____
_____
_____
_____
_____
_____
_____
_____
_____
_____

Day 3 - Fret for nothing

Scripture Reading: "Be careful for nothing; but in every thing by prayer and supplication with thanksgiving let your requests be made known unto God. And the peace of God, which passeth all understanding, shall keep your hearts and minds through Christ Jesus."

(Philippians 4:6-7)

Have you ever wanted something so bad from God you found yourself waiting anxiously? As a result, you thought about receiving His goodness day in and day out that you literally neglected everything else.

Our scripture today tells us to fret for nothing, but pray about everything! It tells us in doing so, God will give us a peace others cannot understand (Isaiah 26:3), and He will guard our hearts against all harm and danger.

God will guard you

I love the word *guard*. It is defined as a precautionary measure warding off impending danger, damage, or injury. Isn't that good to know? God is listening to your prayer requests, providing you peace and protecting you from any danger a premature prayer approval is certain to cause! In James 1:12 it states, "For when he has been approved, he will receive the crown of life which the Lord has promised to those who love Him."

No matter what, be consistent

Throughout life, there are three stages you may find yourself in. Waiting, receiving, or moving to the next stage in your life's journey. No matter what stage you are in, it is important to be consistent throughout.

Daily Prayer: Heavenly Father, we come to You today worshipping You in spirit and truth (John 4:23-24). We thank You for allowing us to see another day with You. We thank You for Your goodness and ask You to humbly bless our prayer requests (declare your prayer requests). We thank You for providing us with peace and understanding, and more importantly, for guarding our hearts. We know we do not have to worry because You are working out everything on our behalf (Romans 8:28). We thank You for doing so and declare and decree it is done. In the name of Jesus Christ of Nazareth, we pray (John 14:14). Amen.

Reflection: Think back to when you were waiting anxiously for an answer to your prayer and you decided to stand on faith and let go and let God. Can you recall when He moved mountains just to meet your needs? Whatever you are concerned about today, let go and watch your faith move the mountains in your life.

Notes:

_____

_____

_____

_____

_____

_____

_____

_____

_____

_____

_____

_____

_____

_____

_____

_____

_____

_____

_____

_____

_____

_____

_____

_____

_____

_____

_____

_____

_____

_____

_____

Day 4 - Day of contentment

Scripture Reading: "Not that I speak in respect of want: for I have learned, in whatsoever state I am, therewith to be content. I know both how to be abased, and I know how to abound: everywhere and in all things I am instructed both to be full and to be hungry, both to abound and to suffer need."

(Philippians 4:11-12)

"This is only a test!" So often, we hear these words during the late night hours via our televisions. Please understand these great words can also be applied to our lives as well. Each and everyday as we go through the journey of life, God is testing us to see if we are ready for a promotion. As a result, we are often confronted by trials and tribulations where God is testing us to see how we will respond. Remember, this is only a test! "Be not afraid of sudden fear, neither of the desolation of the wicked, when it cometh. For the Lord shall be thy confidence, and shall keep thy foot from being taken" (Proverbs 3:25-26).

Praise at all times

He has already promised to see us through. Will you stay consistent and content when adversities come knocking at your door? Or will everyone around you know you are going through an unfortunate event? God wants you to rejoice when you are being blessed and also when you are facing a trial (Acts 16:25-26).

God will make a way

He promises when you go through the fires of life you will be unharmed, just as He has helped Shadrach, Meshach, and Abednego (Daniel 3). God wants the same for you. Do you believe today He is making a way for you and destroying your mountains? In Isaiah 45:2, the Lord states, "I myself will prepare your way, leveling mountains and hills. I will break down bronze gates and smash their iron bars." We have to stay in a place trusting and believing through prayer things will work out. Do not keep your eyes on your issues, but on God. In doing so, He promises you will not be cast down (Psalm 37:24).

Daily Prayer: Heavenly Father, we come to You today worshipping You in spirit and truth (John 4:23-24). We know You have already worked things out on our behalf. Therefore, we can offer You our praises! God, it does not matter how it looks, we know You will turn things around (Philippians 1:12). As we go through trials and tribulations, we pray they will not grieve us, but only make us stronger so we can encourage others who need a Word in due season (1 Chronicles 4:9-10). God, we are declaring the devil's tricks, tactics and schemes have been destroyed this day and will return back to the pits of hell where they belong. We are standing firm on Your Word knowing we are blessed, renewed, and content with what You will do in our lives. We declare we will be blessed more than our hearts and minds could ever imagine (Ephesians 3:20). In the name of Jesus Christ of Nazareth, we pray (John 14:14). Amen.

Reflection: Begin today declaring whatever comes your way, whether good or bad, you will continue to rejoice knowing He is already fighting for you. What things are you rejoicing for today?

Notes:

_____
_____
_____
_____
_____
_____
_____
_____
_____
_____
_____
_____
_____
_____
_____
_____
_____
_____
_____
_____
_____
_____
_____
_____
_____
_____
_____
_____
_____
_____
_____
_____
_____

Day 5 - Wait on the Lord

Scripture Reading: "Wait on the Lord; be of good courage, and He shall strengthen thine heart: wait, I say, on the Lord!"

(Psalm 27:14)

If you are at a place in your life where you are tired of being sick and tired, today you have to commit to wait on the Lord. As our scripture reads, if you declare today you will wait on Him, you will have a sense of peace and renewed strength.

Yield to His Word

Many times in our lives, our battles wear us down, because we are moving at our own speed. Our "to do lists" tend to grow longer and our time with our Master only grows shorter. God promises in His Word, if we yield, wait on Him to move, He promises He is good to those who wait on Him!

In Lamentations 3:25-26, it tells us the Lord is good to those who wait on Him and to the soul that continues to seek Him. It advises us to continue to quietly wait and hope in our Lord.

As you wait, He will direct you

One of my favorite passages in the Bible is found in John 21. It speaks of fishermen who toiled all night but caught nothing. Giving up, they decided to call it quits. Jesus appeared to them and instructed them to cast their nets out to the right side of the ship. They caught so much it was difficult to carry it in! If you wait on Him, He will not only be good to you but you will prosper beyond what you can ever imagine!

Change your strategy

If you have been doing the same old thing you are destined to get the same result. Acts 3:2-7describes a man who had been lame since birth. Throughout his life, he would lay in front of the temple asking for money. Peter and John, upon seeing this man, instructed him to arise and walk in Jesus' name and immediately he did! What can you do differently today? Have you been battling the same issues for quite a while or a long time? Declare you are arising and walking today!

Daily Prayer: Heavenly Father, we come to You today worshipping You in spirit and truth (John 4:23-24). We thank You for renewing our strength today knowing Your goodness will prevail. We thank You for directing our paths so our outcomes are better and our strategies have been God approved. We ask You to continue to guide us so we do not move ahead of You. We stand behind You and wait patiently for Your plans and purpose to be revealed to us as we move towards our destiny. We thank You for all You have done and declare this time we will obtain victory because we have decided not to move at our pace but Yours. In the name of Jesus Christ of Nazareth, we pray (John 14:14). Amen.

Reflection: If you are facing a challenge you have been battling for quite a while, make a decision today to wait for Him to carry you through. Like my mother says, "Lets just wait and see what God's going to do!"

Notes:

_____
_____
_____
_____
_____
_____
_____
_____
_____
_____
_____
_____
_____
_____
_____
_____
_____
_____
_____
_____
_____
_____
_____
_____
_____
_____
_____
_____
_____
_____
_____
_____

Day 6 - Standing up to adversities

Scripture Reading: "What time I am afraid, I will trust in thee. In God, I will praise His word in God I have put my trust, I will not fear what flesh can do unto me."

(Psalm 56:3-4)

How will you react when difficulties come your way? Will you begin fearing what man can do or will you look at your adversary straight in the eye and stand on God's Word? Just as our scripture reads, we have to trust God no matter how it looks and fear nothing or no one.

Rejoice

"Rejoice in the Lord always. Again, I will say, rejoice" (Philippians 4:4)! The Word tells us to rejoice no matter what. Of course you are not rejoicing because you are facing a trial, but simply rejoicing because God is in control and He promises He will do what He says He will do. "My brethren, count it all joy when you fall into various trials, knowing that the testing of your faith produces patience. But, let patience have its perfect work, that you may be perfect and complete, lacking nothing" (James 1:2-4 NKJV). So, count it all joy because God is up to something!

His words are true

In Ezekiel 12:28 it states, "There shall none of my words be prolonged any more, but the word which I have spoken shall be done, saith the Lord God." You too can rejoice knowing not only will God work on your behalf, but He also promises to do it speedily. He said on this day it is done! There is no reason to be concerned or worried, because God is in control. On this day, stand up to your issues, and greet them with a smile because we know God promises to fight our battles on our behalf.

Daily Prayer: Heavenly Father, we come to You today worshipping You in spirit and truth (John 4:23-24). God, You know what we are facing today and for that reason, we ask You to go before us, make all of our crooked places straight and level mountains that are blocking our views (Isaiah 45:2). God, we declare no weapon formed against us shall prosper (Isaiah 54:17) and we declare You have already made our enemies our footstool (Matthew 22:44). God, we declare this battle is already won because it is not ours but Yours (2 Chronicles 20:15). We stand today tall against everything that has come against us and declare the Word of God because Your Word is powerful as a sword (Hebrews 4:12). God, we know we can rejoice because the battle has already been won and Your promises will be fulfilled immediately. God, although we may not understand, we will not lean to our own understanding, but trust You know what is best for us (Proverbs 3:5). We declare we are victorious and prosperous. In the name of Jesus Christ of Nazareth, we pray (John 14:14). Amen.

Reflection: Think on a time when God fought a battle on your behalf. How did you know it was God? Did it seem impossible initially? How did you feel after your victory?

Notes:

_____
_____
_____
_____
_____
_____
_____
_____
_____
_____
_____
_____
_____
_____
_____
_____
_____
_____
_____
_____
_____
_____
_____
_____
_____
_____
_____
_____
_____
_____

Day 7 - Remain quiet during your storms

Scripture Reading: "Be still, and know that I am God: I will be exalted among the heathen, I will be exalted in the earth."

(Psalm 46:10)

Many times when we go through trials, we tend to immediately pick up the phone, speak with a friend or update our status bar to determine what to do. Before long, everybody knows you are going through it. You are no longer walking around with zeal, but wearing a ton of problems on your face. You seek the help of others before seeking the help of God.

Be still and quiet

I have to give credit to my uncle for the material for this day of the fast. He is a very quiet man and most often when he faces trials our family never knows. More importantly, he walks in joy consistently. It is only after he is victorious; he shares his testimony with us.

As our scripture reads today, be still and know He is God! It is important to understand you do not have to consult others without consulting Him first. He will tell you whom to call, where to go or to simply be quiet and He promises to work for you.

Call upon Him

In Psalm 50:15 it states, "And call upon me in the day of trouble: I will deliver thee, and thou shalt glorify me." You can begin to rejoice because it says in His Word; He will deliver you in the day of trouble! In Psalm 72:4 it states,

"He shall judge the poor of the people, He shall save the children of the needy, and shall break in pieces the oppressor." So, there is no longer a need to worry. He says He will fight for you and tear those who have oppressed you into pieces!

Daily Prayer: Heavenly Father, we come to You today worshipping You in spirit and truth (John 4:23-24). We thank You for allowing us to know we do not have to empty our minds to others but can call upon You (Psalm 50:15) and You will deliver us from our oppressors. We know it gets tempting at times, but God You have already worked it out. So now, if we speak on it, it is only for testimony purposes or to encourage someone to stay strong and hold on. We know we can be still, consistent and content because You have already delivered us from our issues, challenges, and oppressors. We thank You for Your mercy and for being a compassionate ruler over our lives. We thank You for supplying all of our needs and blessing us today with constant and powerful breakthroughs. In the name of Jesus Christ of Nazareth, we pray (John 14:14). Amen.

Reflection - If you are facing a situation in your life, make a sound decision to keep the trial to yourself. Pray over it with God, recite and meditate on His scriptures and then and only then after the trial has passed share it with others in the form of a testimony.

Notes:

_____
_____
_____
_____
_____
_____
_____
_____
_____
_____
_____
_____
_____
_____
_____
_____
_____
_____
_____
_____
_____
_____
_____
_____
_____
_____
_____
_____
_____

Day 8 - Keep praying no matter what

Scripture Reading: *"And he spake a parable unto them to this end, that men ought always to pray, and not to faint."*

(Luke 18:1)

Our scripture reading for today, says no matter what, you have to keep praying. I can recall a time when I was deeply worried about a person lying about me to others. I prayed and finally decided I had enough, so I simply stopped praying about it.

Keep praying

One morning, God began to deal with me. He made it quite clear to continue to pray about the person. Not understanding, because of course, I had dealt with it for so long, I began to believe it was simply going to be this way for the rest of my life. Be careful not to believe the lies of the devil! But, out of obedience, I decided to pray about the situation once more. Do you know, shortly afterwards, God revealed this person's lies and evil intentions to everyone? He not only brought the situation to an end, but He led me to Exodus 14:13 and promised me I would see this person no more.

It will turn around

Let me assure you, things will and can turn around. The scripture says, "For I know that this shall turn to my salvation through your prayer, and the supply of the Spirit of Jesus Christ" (Philippians 1:19).

It does not matter how it looks today or even how it feels.

God promises in His Word through prayer, things will certainly turn around. We know this is true because in Isaiah 55:11 it states, "So shall my word be that goeth forth out of my mouth: it shall not return unto me void, but it shall accomplish that which I please, and it shall prosper in the thing whereto I sent it."

If there is ever a time to really pray and believe, it is when you have been counted out, a relationship looks dead, an opportunity seems too far to obtain or something seems hopeless! Make a commitment to keep praying!

Daily Prayer: Heavenly Father, we come to You today worshipping You in spirit and truth (John 4:23-24). We thank You for being true to Your Word, knowing it will not return void. We thank You in advance for turning situations around and raising dead situations to life. No matter what we face today, we can declare and decree we will be prosperous, obtain victory and more importantly be successful. Today, we do not have to believe the lies of the devil or expect things will stay the same, because we know Your Word can change things. We declare and decree the salvation of our loved ones, financial blessings, good health, blessed families and unity. We can trust if we stay in the Word, You will give us the desires of our hearts (Psalm 37:4). In the name of Jesus Christ of Nazareth, we pray (John 14:14). Amen.

Reflection: Have you been dealing with a situation for a period of time? I challenge you to continue to pray about the situation and no matter how hard it looks, God will turn it around in His time.

Notes:

_____
_____
_____
_____
_____
_____
_____
_____
_____
_____
_____
_____
_____
_____
_____
_____
_____
_____
_____
_____
_____
_____
_____
_____
_____
_____
_____
_____
_____

Day 9 - Preparation reduces worry

Scripture Reading: "And at midnight there was a cry made, Behold, the bridegroom cometh; go ye out to meet him. Then all those virgins arose, and trimmed their lamps. And the foolish said unto the wise, Give us of your oil; for our lamps are gone out. But the wise answered, saying, Not so; lest there be not enough for us and you: but go ye rather to them that sell, and buy for yourselves. And while they went to buy, the bridegroom came; and they that were ready went in with him to the marriage: and the door was shut."

(Matthew 25:6-10)

Whatever it is you are hoping and expecting, it is important to be prepared for it. How can you say, one day I will do this or that, but are lacking to put yourself in a position to be able to receive it? In Jeremiah 31:17, God says there is hope in your future. This lets us know the very thing you are hoping shall come to pass.

Prepare and expect

In our scripture reading, there are ten women who set out on a journey - all expecting to meet the bridegroom to attend a marriage. There is something very powerful about this passage -ALL TEN WERE EXPECTING! So, if all ten were expecting to meet the bridegroom, why is it only half were prepared?

A chosen few

Many times when we set out on our journeys with hopes, aspirations and dreams we may all start at the same place, but only a selected few obtain victory because of simply preparing in advance.

So, what are you expecting from God today? Is it success on your job, a long and healthy life, a marriage, financial success or simply peace? You have to begin to not only believe, but also start preparing yourself today.

Daily Prayer: Heavenly Father, we come to You today worshipping You in spirit and truth (John 4:23-24). We thank You first for just being with us. We know no matter what, we can count on You to help us in our times of need and simply be a listening ear when we need a friend. God, we know if we lack wisdom, You will give it to us liberally (James 1:5). For this reason, we ask You to help us to be prepared for whatever lies ahead. Please allow us to make the necessary preparations for ourselves, family, finances, spiritual decisions, careers and any other issues that may have an impact on our lives. We declare we are now moving into an area where we are not only prepared for our blessings, but You are giving us Your grace to make us strong (Romans 4:16). In the name of Jesus Christ of Nazareth, we pray (John 14:14). Amen.

Reflection: Take time today to list five things you have been expecting and praying for from God. Next to each item, list what preparations you can begin to take in order to be prepared to receive it.

Notes:

_____
_____
_____
_____
_____
_____
_____
_____
_____
_____
_____
_____
_____
_____
_____
_____
_____
_____
_____
_____
_____
_____
_____
_____
_____
_____
_____
_____
_____
_____

Day 10 -It's not always going to be this way

Scripture Reading: "Therefore it is of faith, that it might be by grace; to the end the promise might be sure to all the seed; not to that only which is of the law, but to that also which is of the faith of Abraham; who is the father of us all, (As it is written, I have made thee a father of many nations,) before him whom he believed, even God, who quickeneth the dead, and calleth those things which be not as though they were."

(Romans 4:16-17)

Even if it looks like the odds are stacked against you, if you only believe, I promise it will not always be this way. In our scripture, it tells us through our faith and His grace the promise will be fulfilled for all believers. It also tells us, for it is not because of our good deeds or even our bad ones, but because of His grace we will receive the promise.

Never give up

Growing up in a single parent home, I know firsthand how things can change. I witnessed my mother making many sacrifices to make ends meet. She constantly believed we would succeed no matter what. For this reason, she never gave up on us.

After a while, her prayers were answered. My siblings and I each graduated from college as an attorney, professor, nurse and engineer. Consistently, God has continued to bless her financially, physically and spiritually. These days, she does not have to worry about making ends meet. In fact, she often blesses us!

Declare and decree

The second verse of our scripture reading states to declare what you are expecting from God no matter how it looks right now. So, whatever you are expecting to turn around put the words into the atmosphere. Declare dead situations have now risen. Know death and life are in the power of the tongue. Begin to recite scriptures that relate to your situation daily.

Daily Prayer: Heavenly Father, we come to You today worshipping You in spirit and truth (John 4:23-24). God, we know whatever we are facing today will change according to Your Word. We do not have to be dismayed or fearful, because we know even as we pray You are working on our behalf. We expect the promises of Your Word to be fulfilled and we thank You for covering us with Your grace and mercy. The issue of (declare your burdens) we will see no more (Exodus 14:13). For You are working it out for our good! We declare and decree (enter your petitions) it will manifest and more importantly we will utilize it for Your glory. We thank You for all You have done. In the name of Jesus Christ of Nazareth, we pray (John 14:14). Amen.

Reflection: Think about your journey in life and what God has saved you from. Meditate on how God has rescued you from these times. Know because He is such an awesome God, He will do it again!

Notes:

_____
_____
_____
_____
_____
_____
_____
_____
_____
_____
_____
_____
_____
_____
_____
_____
_____
_____
_____
_____
_____
_____
_____
_____
_____
_____
_____
_____
_____
_____
_____
_____
_____

Day 11 - And suddenly

Scripture Reading: "And at midnight Paul and Silas prayed and sang praises unto God, and the prisoners heard them. And suddenly there was a great earthquake, so that the foundations of the prison were shaken, and immediately all the doors were opened, and every one's bands were loosed."

(Acts 16:25-26)

Just recently, God instructed me to praise Him for things I have been praying for. He said, "No longer pray for these petitions as if it has not happened, but begin to praise as if it has already happened!"

For a stronger confirmation, I opened my Bible, and my eyes fell on the scripture reading above and I knew God was once again speaking to me.

Praise Him in the valleys

The scriptures speak of Paul and Silas who were put into jail for merely performing the great works of God. The act of being placed in jail represents the trials and tribulations we too face today. The key behind the scriptures informs us Paul and Silas did not view their current situation as hopeless, but they praised God for what He was going to do. They praised God with such an awesome power that all the prisoners throughout the jail heard their praise.

And suddenly

Suddenly! The scripture tells us suddenly, there was a great earthquake, the prison began to shake and all the doors opened and each prisoner's band loosened. The word *suddenly* is defined as something happening quickly. If you want to see God make big changes in your life, begin to praise Him big and immediately God will begin to work on your behalf!

Start now to praise God in advance. And suddenly, you will see your mountains being leveled and your crooked places made straight (Isaiah 45:2)!

Daily Prayer: Heavenly Father, we come to You today worshipping You in spirit and truth (John 4:23-24). We praise You for whom You are and what You are going to do in our lives. God, we stand on Hebrews 11:6, which reminds us without faith, it is impossible to please You. God, we stand in faith knowing our promises will come to pass. God, we do not care how it looks but we thank You right now for how it is going to look in the future. In the name of Jesus Christ of Nazareth, we pray (John 14:14). Amen.

Reflection: I challenge you to begin to praise God for prayers you expect to come to pass! And suddenly, you will see God do a big thing in your life.

Notes:

_____
_____
_____
_____
_____
_____
_____
_____
_____
_____
_____
_____
_____
_____
_____
_____
_____
_____
_____
_____
_____
_____
_____
_____
_____
_____
_____
_____
_____
_____
_____
_____

Day 12 - Problems are temporary

Scripture Reading: "For our light affliction, which is but for a moment, worketh for us a far more exceeding and eternal weight of glory; While we look not at the things which are seen, but at the things which are not seen: for the things which are seen are temporal; but the things which are not seen are eternal."

(2 Corinthians 4:17-18)

Whether it is a bad relationship, a loved one has been called home, or financial distress, there are certain to be moments in life where you ask God, "Why?"

Being used for God

God could be using us to help someone else. There are many disappointments in my life that have actually turned out to be blessings for others. Because of these experiences, I am now in a position to help others who may be experiencing similar issues and I am able to see them to victory, with God's help. In 2 Corinthians 12:9, He reminds us His grace alone is sufficient. So, no matter what you are going through, God promises to see you through - gracefully.

Only for a moment

I want to let you know you can rejoice, because problems are only temporary. The Word says affliction is just for a moment (2 Corinthians 4:17). Another scripture reads joy cometh in the morning (Psalm 30:5)! No matter what you are going through, you have to remain steadfast, trusting and believing God's Word is the same yesterday, today and tomorrow (Hebrews 13:8). In His Word, He promises He will never leave you or forsake you (Hebrews 13:5).

Trust His strategy not your own

We all have our own plans. We all know where we want to be this time next year, and know, if it is God's will, you will certainly be there, however if it is not, He will lead you another way - a better way. No, sometimes we do not understand it. Proverbs 3:5 states lean not to your own understanding, but to His. You must understand, life is like a long road, and your eyes can only see so far ahead. Isn't it good to know God can see all the way down the road?

So, when life takes you for an unexpected turn or things do not quite work out the way you envisioned, stand still and know God still cares for you. Lift up your hands and continue to pray because one day you will be able to say, "God, I thank You for seeing me through this."

Daily Prayer: Heavenly Father, we come to You today worshipping You in spirit and truth (John 4:23-24). God, we know it is just a matter of time for You to turn this situation around. Heavenly Father, help us not to focus on the seen but continue to focus on the unseen. We declare and decree problems are temporary, but Your glory will endure forever! God help us to keep praying, pushing, and placing our eyes on You. In the name of Jesus Christ of Nazareth, we pray (John 14:14). Amen.

Reflection: Close your eyes and imagine your victory. Begin to praise God as if it has already happened! It will manifest.

Notes:

_____
_____
_____
_____
_____
_____
_____
_____
_____
_____
_____
_____
_____
_____
_____
_____
_____
_____
_____
_____
_____
_____
_____
_____
_____
_____
_____
_____

Day 13 - Consider your ways

Scripture Reading: "Now therefore thus saith the Lord of hosts; Consider your ways. Ye have sown much, and bring in little; ye eat, but ye have not enough; ye drink, but ye are not filled with drink; ye clothe you, but there is none warm; and he that earneth wages earneth wages to put it into a bag with holes."

(Haggai 1:5-6)

In our scripture reading, it speaks of a person who is attempting to live right, but there is a certain area of his or her life, which does not align with the Word of God. You have to ask God to reveal to you both sins, known and unknown, that may hinder your prayers from being answered. Although you may live a Christian life, if you choose to obey God in some areas of your life without obeying Him in other areas, your life will flourish only partially.

Moving to His agenda

As you continue to grow in God, your desires will soon align with His will and purpose for your life. You will have a stronger desire to please Him.

This process requires diligently seeking Him each and every day, keeping His commandments and getting to know His Word. It is only because of our lack of communication with God we fail to understand where He wants us to be. Commit today to take time to listen to what He has in store for you. Remember, it is never too late to start again.

Acknowledge your sins

"I will go and return to my place, till they acknowledge their offence, and seek my face: in their affliction they will seek me early" (Hosea 5:15). This scripture states He will go away until His people acknowledge Him and seek Him. "If my people, which are called by my name, shall humble themselves, and pray, and seek my face, and turn from their wicked ways; then will I hear from heaven, and will forgive their sin, and will heal their land" (2 Chronicles 7:14). Once you acknowledge all of your sins and turn away from them, it is then and only then, God will begin to hear your prayers.

Daily Prayer: Heavenly Father, we come to You today worshipping You in spirit and truth (John 4:23-24). We ask You to search our hearts and make it clear to us whatever areas of our lives that are not pleasing to You. We begin to acknowledge each sin and turn away from our wicked ways. God, we ask You to remove any curse or generational curses, which may have been placed on our lives. We ask You to close any holes in our pockets so we have more than enough. God, we ask You to please return to us and heal our land. We come to You humble and believe we are made new in You today. In the name of Jesus Christ of Nazareth, we pray (John 14:14). Amen.

Reflection: Ask God to reveal anything to you that does not align with His Word. Ask the Holy Spirit to help you to be obedient in all areas of your life. Stand on faith knowing you will begin to live God's way (Hebrews 11:6).

Notes:

_____
_____
_____
_____
_____
_____
_____
_____
_____
_____
_____
_____
_____
_____
_____
_____
_____
_____
_____
_____
_____
_____
_____
_____
_____
_____
_____
_____
_____
_____
_____
_____

Day 14 - Keep your hope in the Lord

Scripture Reading: "It is good that a man should both hope and quietly wait for the salvation of the Lord."

(Lamentations 3:26)

So often, we want to move at our own pace but fail to move at God's. God makes it clear that whatever you desire of Him, if you keep your hope in Him, He will renew your strength.

Sometimes waiting on God can be challenging. We are saying, "God when? God why? God, what are you doing with me? God, I don't quite understand it."

No good thing will be withheld from you

It is not for us to know when, why or even to understand His plans for our lives. It is more relevant to understand He loves us so much He will not leave or forsake us (Hebrews 13:5). He even loves us so much that He will not hurt us and He only desires the best for us. He will not withhold anything good from us (Psalm 84:11). Isn't this great to know? God is like a virus protector. If something does not meet His standards, He will make certain it does not come your way!

There is hope

If you find yourself waiting on God today, stand on His Word. He says there is hope in your future (Jeremiah 31:17). Just hold on, knowing you will live a full life here on earth. Wait for Him and quietly place all of your hope in the Lord (Lamentations 3:26). In doing so, He will provide you with the strength to keep going and give you victory.

Daily Prayer: Heavenly Father, we come to You today worshipping You in spirit and truth (John 4:23-24). Father, we come to You today thanking You for protecting us from both seen and unseen harm. God we thank You for being such an awesome God. We know You will supply all of our needs and give us the desires of our hearts according to Your will and purpose for our lives. God, we know we do not need to worry and we rebuke the devil for attempting to make us hurry along. We know if we wait on You everything will be done in proper and decent order. Also, we understand we do not need to lean to our own understanding, but to Yours. God, while we may not know why or how, we do know You will come through. For this reason, we believe and expect goodness will come our way. So, for this reason, we say thank You. In the name of Jesus Christ of Nazareth, we pray (John 14:14). Amen.

Reflection: If there is something you have been waiting for from the Lord, begin to declare right now God is working it out for you and it will come in God's time!

Notes:

_____
_____
_____
_____
_____
_____
_____
_____
_____
_____
_____
_____
_____
_____
_____
_____
_____
_____
_____
_____
_____
_____
_____
_____
_____
_____
_____
_____
_____

Day 15 - Whose report are you going to believe?

Scripture reading: "I will praise thee; for I am fearfully and wonderfully made: marvelous are thy works; and that my soul knoweth right well."

(Psalm 139:14)

Often in life, you will hear the devil speak to you, saying things like you are too fat, too skinny, too poor, not smart or even not beautiful enough. You must recognize these voices are of the devil.

God had a plan for me

See, I understand what you are going through. I too used to listen to these voices and what is even worse, started to believe them. God already had a plan for my life, I mean a big plan beyond my thoughts. The devil knew if I believed the lies he had construed in my head, it would stop me from moving into the direction God already had for me. God knew my future and more importantly He deemed I would have success.

In Jeremiah 29:11 it states, "For I know the thoughts that I think toward you, saith the Lord, thoughts of peace, and not of evil, to give you an expected end."

Fight back with God's Word

"For the word of God is quick, and powerful, and sharper than any two-edged sword, piercing even to the dividing asunder of soul and spirit, and of the joints and marrow, and is a discerner of the thoughts and intents of the heart" (Hebrews 4:12).

When those voices come against you, you have to fight back with the Word of God. It is the most powerful weapon you will ever own. Therefore, it is important to memorize the Word and be able to recite it immediately. You may find yourself in situations where your Bible may not be near and in order to obtain success, you must quickly fight back with the Word (Joshua 1:8).

Put it in the atmosphere

Make a commitment you will no longer allow the lies of the devil to linger. Declare God's Word and you will win each and every time.

Daily Prayer: Heavenly Father, we come to You today worshipping You in spirit and truth (John 4:23-24). We thank You for being true to Your Word, knowing it will not return void! We thank You in advance for turning situations around and raising dead situations to life. No matter what we face today, we can declare and decree, we will be prosperous, obtain victory and more importantly, become successful. Today, we do not have to believe the lies of the devil or expect things will stay the same, because we know Your Word can change things. We declare and decree the salvation of our loved ones, financial blessings, good health, blessed families and unity. We can trust if we stay in Your Word You will give us the desires of our heart (Psalm 37:4)! In the name of Jesus Christ of Nazareth, we pray (John 14:14). Amen.

Reflection: Whose report will you believe? Have you received any negative reports lately? Speak against these reports, proclaiming the powerful Word of God.

Notes:

_____
_____
_____
_____
_____
_____
_____
_____
_____
_____
_____
_____
_____
_____
_____
_____
_____
_____
_____
_____
_____
_____
_____
_____
_____
_____
_____
_____
_____
_____
_____

Day 16 - Trust Him even when you can't trace Him

Scripture Reading: "Trust in the Lord with all thine heart; and lean not unto thine own understanding."

(Proverbs 3:5)

Sometimes, we face life's issues and wonder why God has not stepped in to help. Perhaps He has already helped us, but we may not see it yet. Even more so, we do not know how God intends to work out our issues because it is not how we expected it.

Lean not to your understanding

When we don't quite understand what is going on in our lives it is important to put it in God's hands. Just as our scripture reading tells us, lean not to our own limited understanding, but stand confident knowing we can both trust and depend on God.

Do you believe He is working it out for your good? I promise He is. And when this trial is over, you will understand, with the help of the Holy Spirit, God's wisdom and knowledge for your life.

Trust Him no matter what

Begin today letting God know you trust Him no matter what it looks like. God knows when to step in at the right time and turn things around. Remember, He knows and sees all. Therefore, the direction you desperately want to travel, God may instruct you that it may not be time just yet. Or the person you are praying for may need a little growing first. Whatever it is, God knows best. God will remain faithful. He will bless you when you put it all in His hands, but first you have to trust God.

Daily Prayer: Heavenly Father, we come to You today worshipping You in spirit and truth (John 4:23-24). We stand on Your Word today and declare we trust You with our hearts, minds, bodies and souls. We do not quite understand what You are up to, but we know - You can see and hear all. For that reason, we thank You for protecting us and allowing the Holy Spirit to be our comforter during this time. God we declare we trust You for working this out for our good and surrender to Your ways. In the name of Jesus Christ of Nazareth, we pray (John 14:14). Amen.

Reflection: Declare you will trust Him and let every anxiety, or worry go by surrendering it all to His will.

Notes:

_____
_____
_____
_____
_____
_____
_____
_____
_____
_____
_____
_____
_____
_____
_____
_____
_____
_____
_____
_____
_____
_____
_____
_____
_____
_____
_____
_____
_____
_____

Day 17 - Ask Him to lead you

Scripture Reading: "For I know the thoughts that I think toward you, saith the Lord, thoughts of peace, and not of evil, to give you an expected end. Then shall ye call upon me, and ye shall go and pray unto me, and I will hearken unto you."

(Jeremiah 29:11-12)

It was laid on my heart today to ask God for His guidance and allow Him to lead me. Sometimes in life, we have an idea of how we want our lives to unfold, but God already knows what is in our future. In our scripture reading, it states God already has a plan for our lives. We simply need to ask Him to reveal it to us, get on board and trust Him to be our source and light!

Ask for direction

Today, I had a conversation with my mother and this thought really came to light. Our conversation was really like no other. Out of the blue, (or should I say God purposed her) she spoke to me about how she chose her career.

My mother stated at the age of eight, she asked God to reveal to her what He wanted her to do. He revealed to her she should be a special education teacher. Having a sister with special needs, she understood the importance of her calling.

He will give you grace

She stated, God gave her grace to perform her job and she

never once regretted her decision. She found herself in situations others would complain about, such as changing young adult students' diapers, keeping students clean, and simply going beyond the call of duty. But, what really stood out is that she enjoyed every minute. While it was a requirement to wear a mask, she chose not to because she wanted her students to know she loved them and had a great deal of compassion for them.

God provided her with the stamina to make it through these times, and when that chapter of her life was over, He revealed to her it was time to move on.

Daily Prayer: Heavenly Father, we come to You today worshipping You in spirit and truth (John 4:23-24). God, we are standing on Your Word today, knowing You will hear our plea. We ask You to order our steps in Your Word. We pray the Holy Spirit continues to lead us and give us the power of discernment, so we can know when to say "yes" and more importantly when to say "no." God, more importantly, help us to recognize when a season has ended in our lives so we can move forward to what You have called us to do. No matter what, let us not look to our past, but continue to press on to a new mark (Philippians 3:13), knowing it is better to end a thing than the beginning thereof (Ecclesiastes 7:8). In the name of Jesus Christ of Nazareth, we pray (John 14:14). Amen.

Reflection: If you are unclear regarding the direction of your life, ask God what does He desire of you. And whatever He reveals to you ask Him for His grace to do His will.

Notes:

_____
_____
_____
_____
_____
_____
_____
_____
_____
_____
_____
_____
_____
_____
_____
_____
_____
_____
_____
_____
_____
_____
_____
_____
_____
_____
_____
_____
_____
_____
_____
_____
_____

Day 18 - Just because it looks like nothing doesn't mean God isn't up to something

Scripture Reading: "And said to his servant, Go up now, look toward the sea. And he went up, and looked, and said, There is nothing. And he said, Go again seven times. And it came to pass at the seventh time, that he said, Behold, there ariseth a little cloud out of the sea, like a man's hand. And he said, Go up, say unto Ahab, Prepare thy chariot, and get thee down that the rain stop thee not."

(1 Kings 18:43-44)

Elijah believed God would end the drought. Therefore, he continued to pray for rain. I bet people thought he was crazy because he kept believing when it really looked like a dead situation. However, he trusted God would stay faithful to His promise.

Persistence is key

We can apply this lesson to our lives today. Are we willing to be persistent and continue to pray in a land of drought? In this passage, we see persistence plus prayer is key. Elijah was not only persistent but he did not take "no" for an answer. Each time his servant came back to report there was no sign of rain he told him to go back a total of seven times before there was even a small sign of a cloud.

Then again

Many times in life we give up too easily – when the doctor says "no," when we have one bad day, an opportunity falls through or our kids are acting a certain way. But, we must realize our prayers are providing a constant and powerful breakthrough. God sent Elijah a small sign – a cloud and soon after there was a heavy rain. Although you may not see huge progress today, God is forming small clouds on your behalf.

Is there an area in your life you have given up in? Are you just another touch away from victory? Stand strong knowing God is forming clouds for you!

Daily Prayer: Heavenly Father, we come to You today worshipping You in spirit and truth (John 4:23-24). God, we thank You for truly listening to our prayers and creating a small cloud in our lives. We can expect, along with the cloud, we will receive a flooding of blessings because of our persistence and attitude of not giving up. We thank You in advance for allowing us to stand on Your Word for our lives and we know everything in Your Word shall come to pass. In the name of Jesus Christ of Nazareth, we pray (John 14:14). Amen.

Reflection: Have you been praying about something and ignoring the small progress? Begin to thank God for the small victories in your life. These small victories will certainly bring about a big movement in the future.

Notes:

_____

_____

_____

_____

_____

_____

_____

_____

_____

_____

_____

_____

_____

_____

_____

_____

_____

_____

_____

_____

_____

_____

_____

_____

_____

_____

_____

_____

_____

_____

Day 19 - Receiving the praises of God

Scripture Reading: "For they loved the praise of men more than the praise of God."

(John 12:43)

In our scripture reading, it speaks of receiving the praise of God and not of man. Most often as we go about our days, we may seek several likes on our social media page, hope to be retweeted on our status bar, or simply wishing friends and family would justify who we are. What is even worse, we also seek the praises from those we do not like, hoping for a "good job," "you are the best" or "I appreciate you" but instead, we should seek the praises of our Heavenly Father.

Follow His will

So, how do we get the praises from God up above? Begin by seeking and implementing God's will for our lives. Love doing what is right and follow His commandments. Let go of any idols you have placed above God, knowing if we follow His will, we will not only have a fulfilled life, but we will obtain the praises of the Heavenly Father.

He has started a good work

In Ephesians 2:10 it states, "For we are His workmanship created in Christ Jesus into good works, which God had ordained that we should walk in them." God expects us to walk into the good work He has already implemented in our lives. We have been created and designed for God's use.

Begin today listening to your heart, asking God how your

life can be used to give Him praise. Cease to live a self-fulfilled life, and let God begin to use you for His purpose. Then you will begin to receive the praises of God.

Daily Prayer: Heavenly Father, we come to You today worshipping You in spirit and truth (John 4:23-24). God, we ask for forgiveness for seeking man's praises and neglecting to seek Your praise. We will no longer put our focus on man, but put our focus on You. We know if we keep our eyes on You, we will not only be blessed, but we will be able to carry out our purpose here on earth. We thank You for no longer allowing us to be in bondage to mankind, but committed to You with our heart, mind, body and soul. We thank You because from this day forward we are no longer seeking man's approval, but Yours alone. In the name of Jesus Christ of Nazareth, we pray (John 14:14). Amen.

Reflection: Ask God today to reveal to you how you can begin to receive His praises in your life.

Notes:

_____
_____
_____
_____
_____
_____
_____
_____
_____
_____
_____
_____
_____
_____
_____
_____
_____
_____
_____
_____
_____
_____
_____
_____
_____
_____
_____
_____

Day 20 - Losing a loved one

Scripture Reading: "When my father and my mother forsake me, then the Lord will take me up."

(Psalm 27:10)

Our scripture reading states, no matter who walks out of your life, God promises to remain. In His Word, we should depend on no one, but stand and lean on God alone. Not your parents, your spouse, children, but only God. "It is better to trust in the Lord than to put confidence in man" (Psalm 118:8).

Let them go

Throughout life, we may lose a loved one or a relationship may come to a sudden end, and we may find ourselves stuck in the moment. If you have been dependent on someone or grieving the loss of a loved one, ask God to see you through. Be determined, no matter what, that you will depend on God during this difficult period in your life. Know your tears are only temporary and there will be a time when you will not have to cry anymore (2 Corinthians 4:17).

It is not God's desire for you to remain there. He desires for you to remove anything holding you back and to trust on Him. For this reason Luke 9:59-60 states, "Follow me!" He also states, "Let the dead bury their dead."

Live again

Sometimes, when we lose a loved one or friend, there is a part of us that dies too. But, begin to ask God to bring this part of your life back.

Let go of your tears. God wants to replace them with joy. Let go of the very moment when you lost your loved one, and leave the past in the past. Know God is doing a new thing in your life. Rejoice now! He is taking everything in your past and turning around for your good (Romans 8:28).

Do you really believe He can? Begin to trust Him and Him alone. I pray you receive this and pray God will do a new thing for you.

Daily Prayer: Heavenly Father, we come to You today worshipping You in spirit and truth (John 4:23-24). God, there have been many people who have come and gone in our lives, but God we thank You for never leaving or forsaking us (Hebrews 13:5). We thank You for those times when we could not count on anyone, when we were able to put all of our trust in You and You saw us through (Psalm 118:8). God, as we continue on this journey, help us to not depend on man and understand all blessings come from You (Psalm 75:7). God, when we feel lonely or down, we can stand on Your Word knowing when no one is standing with us, there You are to give us strength (2 Timothy 4:16-17). Help us to release anyone who we have held in our hearts. Thank You for being all we need and filling in where there are any voids in our lives. In the name of Jesus Christ of Nazareth, we pray (John 14:14). Amen.

Reflection: Ask God today to remove any dependence on people or merely living in the past. Ask God to remove this dependence and fill it with His presence. Remember, God is always there for you.

Notes:

_____

_____

_____

_____

_____

_____

_____

_____

_____

_____

_____

_____

_____

_____

_____

_____

_____

_____

_____

_____

_____

_____

_____

_____

_____

_____

_____

_____

Day 21 - He wants all of you

Scripture Reading: "And thou shalt love the Lord thy God with all thy heart, and with all thy soul, and with all thy mind, and with all thy strength: this is the first commandment."

(Mark 12:30)

For such a long time, I thought giving God most of me was good enough. I thought since I prayed, attended church and would attempt to do what is right, that was enough for God. The reality is, God wants all of our lives, not just a part of it.

Partial obedience = disobedience

What does it mean to give God your all? It means to stop clinching your fists and to stretch out your hands to God. For so long, I put things, people, relationships, and careers over God. I thought if I was a little obedient, or if I took a short cut, I would still receive the promises of God. But, when God says obey, He will not settle for partial obedience. For this reason, anytime I would step out of the will of God, I would immediately be convicted and corrected. But anytime I was obedient, God truly blessed me beyond my belief (Isaiah 1:19).

Surrender

When you decide to give God your all, it requires surrendering every area of your life to Him. Even when it does not make sense, I have learned to obey Him. Do you know what really amazes me? Every time I let go of something, He usually gives it right back, but with lagniappe. *Lagniappe* is a word often used in New Orleans, which means a little something extra!

Obedience is better than sacrifice

I love the passage in the Bible (Genesis 22) that speaks about Abraham preparing to sacrifice his one and only son. As soon as he prepares his son for sacrifice, God exclaims, "Do not lay a hand on the boy," He said. "Do not do anything to him. Now I know that you fear God, because you have not withheld from me your son, your only son" (Genesis 22:12).

The angel of the Lord proclaimed, "I will surely bless you and make your descendants as numerous as the stars...your descendants will take possession of the cities of their enemies, and through your offspring all nations on earth will be blessed, because you have obeyed me" (Genesis 22:17-18). God is no different in our lives. The moment you follow Him, surrender, and let go, God promises He will bless you.

You have to trust that God knows what is best for you. If something is not working in your life, you have to give it up to Him. When you surrender and align your plans with His, it may hurt for a moment, but God will turn your sadness into joy and give you strength (Nehemiah 8:10). You will get to a place and wonder, why didn't I trust God in the first place? He will give you more than your heart could have ever imagined. I promise, you will obtain peace, which the world cannot give to you.

Daily Prayer: Heavenly Father, we come to You today worshipping You in spirit and truth (John 4:23-24). God, we thank You for our twenty-one days of powerful breakthroughs. We declare on this day, we are renewed, refreshed and revitalized. We thank You and praise You for removing anything that has stepped in the way of our relationship with You. On this day, we cast it out and declare Your goodness will follow us all the days of our lives (Psalm 23:6). We believe the Holy Spirit is directing our paths and making things clear to us so we know what direction we should move (1 Corinthians 2:10). We pray when we are unclear about anything, the Holy Spirit will speak to us and give us the power of discernment and truth (John 16:13). We ask You to remove anything, which is unfruitful in our lives, and purge it from us on this day. We only hope to continue to abide in Your goodness (John 15:7). We know we will experience Your kingdom here on earth as it is in heaven (Matthew 6:10). In the name of Jesus Christ of Nazareth, we pray (John 14:14). Amen.

Reflection: Is there an area in your life where you have not been obedient? Ask God to help you to be obedient in this area. Request the Holy Spirit to give you the grace to be obedient. Let the Holy Spirit reveal what steps you should take as you become more like Christ.

Notes:

_____
_____
_____
_____
_____
_____
_____
_____
_____
_____
_____
_____
_____
_____
_____
_____
_____
_____
_____
_____
_____
_____
_____
_____
_____
_____
_____
_____
_____

ACKNOWLEDGMENTS

Many thanks to Robin Kindrick, Allyson Ward and Krishondra Gray, Bianca Carter, Tonya Washington-Nash, James Washington III and Crystal Keeler for their assistance.

ABOUT THE AUTHOR

Growing up in the heart of New Orleans, it is the different spelling of her name, family makeup and unique career path, which makes Kemberley Washington – "Kem." She compares her different experiences in life to a good bowl of gumbo. It may not look so good going in, but simply magical coming out. The good, the bad, and the ugly, she would not change a thing.

Being raised by a single mother who worked as a teacher, failing was not an option. Her mother taught during the day and worked various part-time jobs in the evenings to support her and her three siblings. It is because of her mother's sacrifice early on, her and her siblings are successful today.

In addition to her mother, she also credits her father for who she is today. Her father, who co-owns an architectural firm, Hewitt-Washington & Associates, provided her the opportunity to work as an accounting clerk during her teenage years. After graduating from Southern University and A&M College, she had the opportunity to work with the Internal Revenue Service (IRS) as both a Criminal Investigator and a Revenue Agent. However, after realizing carrying a gun wasn't her thing, she utilized her experiences and pursued the calling on her life - to write and educate. Today, she is often seen on many news stations. She has contributed to *Bankrate.com, FoxBusiness.com, Yahoo Finance, The New Orleans Agenda* and many more. Also, she is the author of *The B.A.D.G.E. Financial Planner, 21 Days of Victorious Living* and *more.* She frequently updates her blogs, *Kemberley.com and 21daysof.com.* She also teaches undergraduate business students at Dillard University.